L.Y.T.E.S. Stages of Life

Quanesha Amangele

Presentation by *BookLeaf Publishing*

Web: www.bookleafpub.com

E-mail: info@bookleafpub.com

ISBN: 9789357617673

First edition 2023

In memory of Adopted Uncle William Lynn McCloud, Uncle by Marriage Len Fairley. Maternal Great Grandparents Oreister "Orretta" Allen Wallace Malloy Smith, Curley Spoon Glover, Frank Leroy Hawkins, and Rosa Walker Williams. Paternal Great Grandparents Alexander "Sandy" McGirt, Annie Bell Jones Leggett, Charlie Chavis McLeod Mcrimmon Smith, and Bessie Baker Brown McLeod Southerland.

ACKNOWLEDGEMENT

For the students of Millbrook High School poetry club, and the former students and supporters of William Peace University spoken word group phenoMEnal.
For my mom Sharon, my father Robert, my auntie Tina, and my best friend Joyce.

PREFACE

While the content of these poems are based on my truth I would not be the person I am without them. To each of you that are mentioned or discussed, thank you for giving a part of my life perspective.

A Young Lover's Plea

What more can I do,
to show you that I really love you.
How much more can I cry,
before you stop calling me a lie.
Who can I tell,
without you putting me through hell.
Where can I cry,
so you will know how hard I try.
When will you allow me to love you,
show you that I will put no one above you.

Blind Puppy Love

I'm in a blind,
Puppy love has taken over my mind.
I really love her can't she see,
there is no other place I'd rather be.
I gave her all of my heart,
from the very start.
I gave all of my love to one person,
without her you can find me nursing.
Without her in my life,
my heart has been cut by a knife.
Why am I still hurting,
I guess to her I was a burden.
Why does this anger last,
when will my memories of her pass.
I could care less if you were my bae again,
but in our friendship we have too much time put
in.
Never will I love the same,
because loving you turned into heartbreak and
pain.
Forever in my heart she will stay,
Lord, give me the strength to start a new day.

Love Note

I miss the feeling of her lips against mine,
i still can't believe I'm talking to a girl this fine.
Could it be that I've reached the top of the line,
the answers will come all in due time.
Will she really be mine,
how did I get a dime.
My love my joy,
her love is not a toy.
But I'm still wishing to call,
her my girl who is above all.
Ugh! I hate waiting,
when can we start dating.
At the end of school we say,
but damn a year later and still no play.
I guess that is because of people and their
mouths,
ready to set fire that can't be doused.
Jump or speak stupid if you want to,
my boo damn sure come before you.

memories of our love

In early October 2010,
that is the day the confusion truly began.
Walking home from school,
it's not too hot and the temps are cool.
She said do you still have those feelings for me,
I say why is it that you are asking me.
She looked at me and smiled,
and I knew she would be worth the while.
We talked and texted everyday,
we got together officially on valentines day.
Always greeted with soft sweet kisses,
No matter what, she will always be my miss.
No one wanted me to be with her,
but with her I thought I had gone upper yonder.
May 21st, it all came to an end, picking up
pieces I didn't know where to begin.
She was my heart my one and only true love,
when it came to her no one was above.
But there are the memories of love.
Now to change my life and focus on the man up
above, and a new found love.
I'm not competing with anyone for what is
rightfully mine,
Baby my fears and wonders with God's love will
all change over time.

Black American

You say that I am average
but I will live longer than your marriage.
Some of us may be affiliated with a gang...
for there is not a color that makes me bang.
My pants sag because I've been hurt.
I don't care anymore...tired of being treated like
dirt.
I talk a lot of trash
because your level I will surpass.
Other races classify me as a fool
but in reality, I am just being cool.
I keep everything real
for time is not something on earth that we have
to kill
I was born unprivileged
now dream of chasing to be a kid rich.
Dr. King said my skin color did not matter.
The world is my ball and I am the batter.
I may be a thug
but I have a heart full of love.
My favorite drink might be Kool-Aid
but you and I together we will both be paid.
In the ghetto I live
'cause it was all my parents had to give.
I've set a new fashion trend
because I am black...and an American.

White American

I am a rich kid...popular
Leader and not a follower.
I may be stuck up
With a drink in my cup.
They made a movie called "White Men Can't
Jump."
You may call me white trash, but I don't live in a
dump.
Yes, it's true...some of us wanna be black
but my skin color doesn't cut me any slack.
My work is done to perfection.
You and I both struggled in this recession.
I may not know how to dance.
So what if I wear size zero in pants?
I have evolved far from a racist.
Everyone get in your places.
You say that I am smart
but you and I both were given the same start.
My kids may be spoiled brats,
While my body may be covered in ink tats.
So what if not all of us are jocks.
but for our generation, it's time to put down the
Glocks.
You and I were born with the power:
To climb up the CEO tower.

For my race, I've set a new education trend....
Because I am white, and I am American.

Letters to my dear 011413

Beautiful in every way, whenever I am feeling bad you know how to brighten up my day. You are my favorite girl, if I could I would give you the world. Maybe it is the gentle, soft and delicate way you play with my hair, I will tell other girls quickly that I don't even care. Sometimes I can't stop staring at your face, in my eyes and in my heart, that's right, you've got that place. You are the only one I see, with you is where I only want to be. To be honest, I am kind of new at this. I want to keep you protected, this feeling was so unexpected. I love feeling this way, I know I have to put in more work before I deserve to call you my bae. For the most part, you've got what the other girls can't have, and I am trying my best not to be a screw-up like Donovan McNabb. I start to blush when I say or think of your name, sometimes I wonder if you feel the same. You are always on my mind, when I came to college I did not know that this would be what I would find. Let my love keep you warm when you are cold, loving the way this bond is being formed and I want it to grow old. Screw my whole meet me halfway thing, I will meet you all the way and all in between. This all seems so strange to me, I like how you do not criticize but keep it 100 with me. I want to love you the way that you want me to, just show me what I have to do. If you teach me how, I will take the vow. To love, honor, and cherish which means my love for you will never perish.

06/20/13

Well our love didn't last long,
crying trying to figure out where everything
went wrong.
The gift deep down on the inside of my gut,
telling me that our time is up.
I did not want to believe it,
devastated me to my pit.
Should have known something when you played
me the first time,
messed around cross-breeding lemons and
created a lime.
But it's all good,
ever since you told me about the old girl, it
sounded like you were blowing smoke from the
wood.
I remember back in 01/14/13, I didn't want to be
a screw-up like Donovan McNabb, now like
Trey Songz and fumbled your heart cause I
couldn't reach out and grab.
Nov 6th, 2012 is when we began but as they say
all great things must come to an end.
However I am starting to pick up the pieces to
be put back together, and I am choosing to be
chased until I meet my forever.

Who will cry

Who will cry for the person, who never got to be called a grad.
Who will cry for the person, whose body lay cold in the middle of the street.
Who will cry for the person, who's just another body bag.
Who will cry for the person, whose family will continue to weep.
Who will cry for the person, whose killer will have those memories to keep.
Who will cry for the person, whose nation will rise in his honor.
Who will cry for the person, whose story will never be told.
Who will cry for the person, whose life was lost at only 17 years old.

I am asking who and I already know who.
God will cry for the person, who never got to be called a grad.
God will cry for the person, whose body lay cold in the street.
God will cry for the person, who's just another body bag.

God will cry for the person, whose family will continue to weep.

God will cry for the person, whose killer will have those memories to keep.

God will cry for the person, whose nation will rise in his honor.

God will cry for the person, whose story will never be told.

God will cry for the person, whose life was lost at only _ _ years old.

What Is Love

Before we can begin to say, feel and understand;
We must know when to take a stand!

A stand that love is just not a word, it is kind of
like that story my mom told me about the bee
and the bird.

No I do not mean the birds and the bees, because
it's not just OK to give away your seeds.

See L Love is legendary, luckily lively and light,
just like the dew in the early mornings' late
hours of the night.

See O lOve is two becoming one 100%, open,
full of optimism and is not always going to be
OK, so we must keep in mind the positive times
that love is made a way.

See V loVe love is vibrant, virtuous, vital and
valued, look for and beyond scanned and found
in the total menu.

See E lovE is earnest, ecstatic, effortless,
electrifying, energizing, engaging, excellent,

exciting and exquisite, if this is what you
possess would you still quit it

Do not give up on love, because it comes truly
from above! Giving up on love occurs when it is
confused with his twin cousin lust, it takes time
to build to it there is no need to rush!

Heaven

A special place prepared for you and me, now
his face I have got to see.
The drum and the trumpet sounded, and around
the room I went.
As the thunder roared and the angels rejoiced,
my flesh in this term has run its course.
Here in paradise there are no burdens or pain, I
am riding the morning train and heaven I have
gained.
My life had been a little tough, but we are all
gathered here because heaven had waited long
enough.

Becoming an Angel

When I see Jesus it will be, just him and me.
If you listen to the earth then you will know, that
I have fought the good fight and reaped what I
have sowed.
He told the wind to blow, and the sun to show.
He told the lightning to flash, and the clouds to
dash.
He told the thunder to sound, and called for the
rain to hit the ground.
He told the moon to shine, to provide light
during nighttime.
He told the insects and animals to appear, as a
reminder to us that all his creations are dear.
Faint not I say unto you, as of my sunset I know
this to be true;
Man that is born of a woman has an appointed
time, accepting him as your savior is the only
way to become an Angel keep that in mind.

Shadows

What is done is permanent just as the sun, on a new journey let us begun.
Each moment that we breathe is already in the past, pick up your halo and get ready to blast.
To an amazing future, all that was done is repaired with one suture.
During this period, be daring, where you will find yourself spending more time self-caring.
Within you and your abilities lies optimisticity, even bad press can boost your publicity.
Although humbleness must be your first willing, or your soul will continue to be a killing. As the moon rises and the sun is setting, when you are living on yourself you are betting.

Let not our hearts be troubled

You believed in God and you believed in Jesus,
You knew that the day would come when you
would leave us.
You were ready and we were not,
We will see you again only if we faint not.

In remembrance of me

When you think of me, think of how full of life
my flesh used to be.
Let that be your reminder that I am with you in
spirit,
Every step of the way because you all are my
dearest.
The light that I carried let it carry you through
this,
Find comfort in knowing that it is only my flesh
that can be missed.
I am still with you,
Because when God saved me he saved you too.

To capture the color of my eyes

Have you ever seen a soul so deep, one would
think. That they were buried under the crust of
the earth,
Every interaction they have they experience a
rebirth.
Have you ever seen a "melanated" person with
freckles,
Their genetic disposition and non traditional
belief brings those that heckle.
Then hides,
but when you looked into those eyes.
You saw the hurt and pain,
you're intrigued now but they question what is it
you want to gain.
Life had been quite difficult for them which they
wore well,
and the conversations leave you with questions
of how people could have put them through hell.
Yet they still walk with and give grace,
It's because they needed it to become the Ace!
It was the trauma that made them wise,
Their pillows are full of silent cries.

From strangers to friends through poetry

Jamecia when I met you almost 10 years ago, I knew you were special but how special I didn't know. But watching you from close and sometimes afar, everyone's life you touch gracefully become a superstar. Your shoulders have felt many people's cries, and your soul's beauty is unhidden even to the untrained eyes. I am extremely thankful to God and your parents for creating you, saving all Aquarius cause you know what I went through. It is truly an honor and a privilege to have you as a friend, you keep me motivated because you believed in me more than I believed in myself when I began. You supported me when I had none, and the countless store runs. Maybe it was because I could steal your blankets and crash on your couch, or maybe it was how quickly you jumped when I said ouch. Maybe it is the Leo rising, or maybe it's the fact that no matter the time, no matter the distance, I know you would ride with me. Or maybe it's because I could fuss with you about doing your hair locked in the room and you paid me no mind or maybe it was all of us packed in my car that one time. Whatever it is,

I'm thankful, cause even when I didn't want to accept you made sure my tank was full.

Mountain Top

I've gone to the mountain top,
I've identified patterns and habits that I need to stop.
Seeing the trees on the sides of the mountain,
they are not leaning over but producing oxygen like a fountain.
Gaining a clear view of having faith beyond a mustard seed,
Germs are not visible to the naked eye yet a disease can breed.
False confidence false self-esteem false sense of one's self,
But this journey can only be described via bass and treble clef.